GHETTO CLAUSTROPHOBIA

Shanta Lee Gander

First Edition 2021 ©Shanta Lee Gander
All rights reserved.
ISBN: 978-1-939728-40-1

Diode Editions
Doha, Qatar
Richmond, VA
Design & layout: Law Alsobrook
Author photo: MacLean Charles Gander

Ordering & Contact information: http://www.diodeeditions.com

GHETTOCLAUSTROPHOBIA

Dreamin of Mama While Trying to Speak Woman in Woke Tongues

For all of us who had to be audacious as we dared to be rising above every past harm, person, place, and thing that tried to tell us we could not

Ghettoclaustrophobia

I

Fugue State: Dreamin of Mama

II

Ghettoclaustrophobic Dreaming

III

Trying to Speak Woman in My Own Tongue

IIII

Fugue-Woke-State

Ghettoclaustrophobia

/ˈgedō klôstrəˈfōbēə/
Whether place people, state of mind,
you be locked in until you don't want to be.

Noun—People
Ghettoclaustrophobics (also Ghettoclaustrophobes, Ghettoclaustrophobians)

1. Any group of people.
   They evade capture.
   They evade description.
2. Identity. Perceived or imagined.

Noun—A Place
Ghettoclaustrophobia

1. Fashioned for, but not by.
   Think characters. Think props.
2. Big, so big. Expansive. Endless.
3. Any place. The place with the matching riding mowers.
   That place where cliques of moms go by the same name.
4. Hotel room, apartment, house.
   Dreamscape, cityscape, ruralscape, selfscape.
   Could be another country.
   Could be the human body as container,
   as shell, as place.
   From block to brick to burb
   to brownstone, to any place.
   As in so many, as in endless.
5. These places,
   real and imagined,
   just like the people,
   they evade capture.

Adjective - State of Mind/States of Being
*Only an ailment if you want it to be.

1. Black girlhood in America
2. Nightmares
3. Stages of human development

I

Fugue State: Dreamin of Mama

The Mother Who Brung Ya' (I)
Mama

I.
A smile from six years ago
faded in the green
of Elizabeth park
Gazebos gave cousins

solace from thorns
and sun, shielding
laughter and secrets
from adults

Girl interrupted
by talk of pussy
smoke fills the nostrils,
while alcohol flushes kidneys

cackles are carried
out of kitchens,
and delivered to the dinner table
Slurred speech is the soundscape

in purple Cadillacs
No real place to go,
you were looking
for yourself. Pieces

of that nineteen-year-old
among the missing
She's in the cesareal scar
across your stomach,

in the bottle of Ms.
Clairol #30,
kidnapped by that gap
between your two front teeth

She's in the apartment
gone wrong with the boy
you've known since
sixteen, the autistic son,

and your adolescent mirror
who shows you your face
before life touched it
Maybe she's

still laying somewhere
on that abortion table
Still wondering
about what happened

to Warehouse Point,
to those times hot
pavement kissed feet
You were chasing Sweet Pea,

but just like you,
she never was

II.
The gum's pop, the chewing
erases sharp pains
and that blood,
that night at Mt. Sinai

like the way television's
volume hid the sound
of falling shower curtains
The police never came

that night, words and
rationality never came
to the strange place
where men hold your hand

I searched for my dignity amid
forced trips to Salvation Army,
those musty racks wrapping us
in the decaying urban

You found yours
in designer imposter perfumes,
Author's Drug lipstick,
I wondered who I'd be

separate from your world
Who would I be in my world
where the tangled yarn in the closet
grows with me?

III.
The way purple was
your favorite color for the way
it reminded you of Prince,
the way a hallway closet

colludes with piled clothing
to hide Café Vienna,
American cheese slices,
pictures taken in places not here

The red tint of your skin
The girlish dimple
between your brows
How your hazel eyes

glittered like glass when angry
How oversized shirts
covered your shame
Fondue with Cousin D.

The scar above the inner part
of your left ankle
The minister runnin church
out of his garage

Bits and pieces, all these things
aid and abet
Do as I say, not as I do.
I lip sync Boys II Men and Tupac

Inventing a mama
I can feel the way you tap me
while talking,
it followed me here

where I keep vigil in my own mirror

Black Book of Creation

I.
How far can you? she said, *far,* he said.
    How far? she said, *so far,* he said, *that*

remembering all of them becomes a chant,
    he said. *I only,* she said,

can go this far, she said, *Great, great, gre...*

II.
Some sounds invite eavesdropping to all
    the befores. Before all the gates of
never return, before tongues couldn't
    be trained in what they no longer are
Before they knew about choosing
    between leaving of will or leaving of force

Before the before that is time
    we didn't call time. Before

there was anything colored about it.
    That is—then, here, and there—are not separate

but on a table

III.
Mother sits fashioning her children.
    Cosmic clay, stardust, and obsidian

for resilience, dreams for seeing,
    and the things not contained by language,
and hardships sometimes cloaked as nightmares
    Story stitched into DNA like

home—distant—multiplied by
    separation anxiety, forgotten becomes exponential force

that becomes a country expanded beyond
    its own self, beyond the shell that holds it together

IV.

Creation is the conversation
What do you want to be? said she

Anything we choose, said we, *But what*,
said she, *because the world*, said she,

will choose if you don't, said she. *Magic*,
the ability to manipulate circumstance,

said we. *It shall be*, said she
Time lords, said we, *to collapse*

and expand time at will, said we,
visibility and invisibility at will, said we

It shall be, said she. *But*, said she,
as gifts are given, they can be stolen,

said she. *So, with each*
of these things, said she, *it shall be*

a veil of forgetting, a spirit
that resists destruction, and these wings, said she,

Do not let anyone tell you
they do not exist. Do not let anyone tell you they are wax!

V.

Funny how the universe beats
against itself creating echoes

How far can you go back? they said, *Far*,
she said, *how far?* they said, *So far*, she said,

It becomes a chant, she said,
I know all the names of my mothers

Dreamin of Mama

Here, Mama be like,
I'm gonna carry your bag
sharing the burden she's put in it

Here, we argue like sisters
screaming the trauma
that created us

We show up
lulled into forgetting
startin where we ended to do it all again

If I arrive awake,
she shows me
how to read the witness marks sayin,

Our bodies
                    the clocks,
Our Mamas

Multiplied by greatness

They be
                    horologists...

The Mother Who Brung Ya (II): Mama Grand

There, you be in your chair
There, I be sitting on the floor,
Both of us facing forward,
clutter collides with our bodies

It's our family, some will say
It grows around us, we ignore it
Just see The Price is Right. Just see the news.
Just see...everything

Weekend refuge
rescue from mama
Middle-of-the-night glow
of Clint Eastwood

In the middle of time, we face forward
You be in your chair, gauze over cataracts once over eyes
I be standing, waiting to hear the horn
you fill my hands with snacks, with money

Words once snatched now appeared superficial,
angling themselves across miles and phone lines
Slipping through the brick, deadbolts,
and my guilt that held all of you

This time I sit facing forward. You, curled in your bed
The doll you hold, you call Mary because she is your oldest sister
This time, we know what we know. Our tongues? Our Language?
Snatched up, missin like our time

We don't stand, we neva did
We be beside each other jus like back in the day
Just like back then, I hold all I couldn't say,
embryonic questions

In the year of no numbers,
I bundle and tie all my tongues of before
for each hour that ghosted us, all silences, and all my faces you never met...
these will help me find you

I bring all these, I sit facing forward
my path lit with all our symbols, all our neva said
When I get there, there be no deadbolt, no brick,
no miles, no mama, no time

...no time

In Search of Lineage

Tattoos threatened serpentine movements
from sacral seats to the lower lumbar
To the base of a soft neck, speaking braille to fingertips
Bimini road on skin declaring provenance

Eyes, lips, nose...faces unplaceable, language unspeakable
Cherokee, Anasazi, Kiowa, maybe Tribes of No Name
S-Curves like that birthed a generation along a caravan
of bought and stolen daughters, deaf to the-wise-women-sign-posts

for cash registers that needed reclamation
How did all this shit become so bad that we forgot good?
Starts with prayers, wish making, hope that is between and betwixt to knowing

Life is the craft of veil make, one day you'll learn to see through it
And your great-great grandmother's grandmother's holy writ,
I was a sacred prostitute.   I am the sacred, profane, and all in between
But when you speak it, it ain't nobody else's lineage

It demands your owning
I spoke fire, its filigree raised as a reminder
hair washed in first rains, a scant mental sketch
Pinehurst or Colorado, maybe it's the farthest I can go back

A gesture, a word, familiar faces   something about
my reflection instructs   I won't forget her
This distance is beyond here to there
Bodies don't become   they are

Tongues don't speak the dead language of what is
while hands craft the jigsaw of pitch Black

Mama & Papa in Daylight

I.
Don't let anyone, he said,
do that to you   *You give respect,*
you get respect
That's it.

Dirt-caked clothes prevent me
from seeing all the ways
they are family. Prevents me
from hearing the son say,
Dad, this happened today...

II.
Mama and me, we were never
in a nail salon, instead,
in banks, in stores,
in Salvation Army   on Church pews

Pinching replaces talking
Glaring substitutes affection
And lips drawn tighter than a cat's asshole...

No teeth
No words
No soothing

If I can make myself small,
I can make myself invisible

III.
The woman with the clipboard,
the father and son conversation,
straightened backs, no down-slouch,
even with my stolen stares, they refuse capture

Instead, stories
Instead questions, *Who were they there for?*
Big family, was it someone's birthday?
I never had a birthday like that
What did the son say
to get that kind of caring?

IV.
I choke on my insults
chase it with assumption,
follow the trail of shards
forcing me to go back,

find my childhood,
find those instances with
my own parents...
Like the dirt in the daylight

of the salon   they are all missing

Forgotten tastes like cheese sour to the tongue while visiting Mother

Here, you banish sins of the day,
    banish what couldn't find its way

into the pot, the rot in the corner,
    a veiled stench. In another there, you be balm,

salve. You be sanctified,
    a part of how good got right, how right got...

*

Us forgot how to get right.
    The closest we come feels kinda like the

voices that reach in, makes we jump,
    not that kinda jump   The one hid in haint blue,

red doors, the one where the pulpit pimps be sayin
    You gotta be ready when he comes rollin up in a chariot

For when he comes,
    you ain't got time to be fussin

He be the boy from that otha place
causin her fuss. Maybe he be like she,

theftin' time. He be that boy from a place
they wouldn't speak bout, both them

letting the world think that their skin
told its kind of truth. It was

a kin's kind of truth. Taste like braille
built upon bodies, white space, ellipses, dashes

Honey, they don't teach that kind of code

*

The code wasn't in a book. Branches
so tangled tongues can't speak it

But mama's mama's mama's mama
claps back from forgotten

Mama's mama's mama's mama standin
at the edge of my bed. She's followed

the yellow traces of the calendula
to my pillow, reaching for my throat

hers filled with daggers, disturbance,
and time sayin, *Girl, you didn't ask*

Mother Who Brung Ya' (III): Some Say

Mama's mama's mama's mama
some kind of medicine woman,

or was it *She made balm,*

she made *for estranged souls.*
A tangled tale on mama's side

bout how all the men lost eaten

How all the men
got no names,

well few,

mama's grandfatha went by Sing,
mama's great granfatha, a full name The women?

They be the kind refusin unknowin

As in they got names. As in
follow the trail of chicken feet

Follow

all the ways we know seein

with our eyes closed.

One of papa's great grandmamas,

a Cherokee woman,
Papa's great grandpapa,

a white man both 'em no name,

Names get lost like that...
but follow they daughter, Betsy

follow the stories...

Her grandchildren tell it
She washed her hair in first rain

On mama's side,

When one of great-grandma Josephine's 16 died,
I wanted to know

How do you make dead tongues speak?

Initial offering
Gratitude

Make space for what you ask

Not as stranger as kin and when you ask
be bound by blood,

and as for the talk part?

The speak?
Notice the way

sentient cinerariums carry the bones,

the way they buzz
between breath and letters,

the bed of their humming

in that one story
mama talked bout the water breaking
She walked opposite of the hospital the night I came
Those bones,
those bones,
they started to chant in that otha story

That story where they sai...

Roaming the Deadlands

His ghost hung in the attic apartment
I was told to bury my face, hide from the naked
Keep one eye open, you'll know what the forms are
They ask, *What did you hear?*

Name nothing. We had no sight, silence
our braille as years do what they do: passing,
gifting, scattering...we still don't know
who started it all off...the first taste of delicious

like the dried blood of meat on tongues
teaching want without why or how. Ghosts hung
along a mapped highway of dead roads, we
became the spirits roaming the topography

What does unfamiliar feel like beyond the senses?
Ghosts of what we were haunting, leaving our skin

of the spode trauma kind

II.

Ghettoclaustrophobic Dreaming

Dreaming

I’m at 280 Collins Street.
Sometimes, on a highway,
on a train—always headed
East

Maybe I’m all these
places incarnate,
the one who evades naming,
the one who refuses
mapping

Syna-ghetto-sthesia: An Exhibition

Materials
Displacement from African Kingdoms
Unknown, Transatlantic Slave Trade,
Miscegenation, Brick, Glass, Cheap Carpet,
Cheap Paint, Redlining, White Flight

It tasted like...

Red brick with bones that tasted like fever.
The length is a forever multiplied by the flat
and hollow of the way pale wheat, thin cheap carpet,
and 1000 watts of muted incandescent leaves longing
on the tongue. Belly empty now hollow,
enough of a skin to stretch and start tappin

Apartment 2C
Chains wrapped and hung round necks, the bodies
dangle from the shine not absent pon ears when
touched to eyes by passing palms. You be
in Mississippi, you be in the whistle that never passed
through lips to touch white female bodies, or you
be in the land of the true true—that walk, no limpin,
no pimpin, deliberate. Eyes that touched forgotten
and made it back in time to show us again. That dip
in that head tho, like they know tho...

Apartment 3D
Bodies the cola of butta, taste like distance taste like
the way we all watched, *You pretty for a dark girl.*
You pretty like Patra. Taste like the skin and
good hair of Myra matched base notes of Nicole's silky
ponytails. As the grown folks said, *They really smellin*
themselves, kinda like the way the other They once said,
These are more valuable than those on the auction block
But that ain't now. Now you be a bridge to tell us where the exit sign is

Ms. Topaz, Ms. 4G
With the family color of slightly burnt sugar cookies
My face helped her touch home, the way missing
closes the space between bodies. Her question
touched my skin then lingered in the hallway
a lil longer

In Between: The Hallway & Apartment 3G

Linger like that song in 3G—that one song bouncing off
bodies and building, all of us listening to a grown man's lullaby

Apartment 2I
Not like the others above, none below, but in a fold,
in the jugular notch of the red brick. In the best one only best because...
the balcony. Vacant because her son hangs somewhere from a place
in here that can't hold the dead weight of a grown man

Apartment 1D
Faint cigarette smells are a soft caramel color
in a silver wig, innocuous, quiet, a petite frail secret

It sounded like....

Permanent press rising off a woman's slip and a man's
work pants in the dryer while Mrs. R is at work
Bitter slight sweet footsteps of the 95% chocolate
non-organic Taza bar and her growing stomach
from a husband gone missing

A Drowning & Apartment 4G Bearing Witness

Materials
A Sunday Morning, A single Mother
with Two Children, and A Grandma with a .22

Mahalia Jackson's voice in 4G, the hallway pounding
with the mother of a baby left alone in a tub, all held
by grits, sausage, and Sunday's morning.

What open car doors and Grandma's .22
pointing at those drunk fools looks like
from the 4th floor later that day

The way rubber and the heat from the engine
from a milk run made over four hours ago stays in the air

Last Scenes of Syna-ghetto-sthesia

Looked like the cacophony of a dude named
after a brand after a sport he'll never play,
the sweet and bitter lemonhead on taste buds
that made girls like me wanna be her,
or wanna be that folding table that held the
the bodies of teen love in the laundry room

The way echoes bounced from bathrooms
from barricades upon faces from a night out
we weren't supposed to see

What *NO* feels like through cheap metal doors,
what *Another Bad Creation* tates like in the Valley
of Lost Kings and blind Queens, or maybe
just a bunch of niggas from around the way

The visible invisible on our bodies,
cars filled and unfilled in the parking lot
of the red brick whose bones tasted like
the fever we caught

Learning Language

I. Symbols & Sounds

We mimicked what we knew
We watched what we couldn't understand

It wasn't a bang but the sound
It wasn't the expansion but the capacity

II. The Phoenician Alphabet

Tables in kitchens keep count, how long does it take
to commit 26 of them to memory?

Sless instead of *mom* for the corner store, for the
way it had everything. Everything meant home

The way *blue* was gifted by autism
gifting the synesthesia we wanted

III. Guttenberg in the Locker

Your writing never looked like that
secrets never seemed so loud

Spiral bound notebooks hid in closets
with birth control, Onyx, and Wu Tang Clan

I was going to hide in her basement,
we had the plan worked out

How many things can you fit into a locker?
The things whose secrets take up no space

IV. Write it, it will come

The street lamps across the way
create what mouths refuse to birth

What do you want
when you grow up?

Freedom
Love
Money

There was a fourth and fifth forgotten
to a curfew and to time

V. 140-Characters

Food can substitute feelings, cats and dogs make you forget.
See family photos: Father Mother Dick Puff, sometimes Sally
See my family

VI. Symbols

We read shadows on screens
not seeing the tea leaves

We are the oracles of new the hieroglyphs,
most fluent in six emoticons

Oumuamua wasn't looking for us,
it was the cave drawing we sent back ourselves

We were warned about the dangers
of knowing ourselves too well

Witness Marks

for the horologists

Figure Drawing

Leather Fuck-Me boots that never stretched
That nail sticking out of the waterbed

Too many times playing on the rug
while silent damage was imprinted on skin

My thighs that caused the friction that caused
his stares that caused pieces to break inside

10 years, being female, and that note
a stranger passed to me in my living room

That kerosene lamp, the way an edge of a counter
is the barrier to a 2-year old learning lust for the first time

Or maybe it was something else
Fodder for muted arguments

between Truth and Legend, like a piano's
edge teaching another kind of lesson

Maybe it started with one drink too many
before she saw results of that storm

What the trees tell us

Keeping company with shrapnel, bark folding a General's
thoughts like sap, *How are we getting out of this?*

From shade to shield to witness, miscegenation's safe here
as we measured time counting backward

from the moment of the broken umbilical cord, multiplied
by each day soft spots close and sight goes missing

In the South, branches be throwin signs against the sky
that became the shadows and geography of our faces

And when you touch it, you know hands,
backs, and bodies have needed this

to be steady,
to be still

Nature's Parameters

Measurement taken and parameters set,
we call it a National Park

Plates move and chunks disappear with
the knowing we never had. To read the space,

follow the bones disguised as hills,
use your feet as fingertips to read the braille

of jagged lines, the paths once roads, listen to the way
buildings sway with water or quakes, watch sulfur

pretend to be contained, watch the way
wild pretends to have distance

Dislocate from the now
Notice how it tells you whose been here

Surviving R. Kelly and Michael Jackson When They Are Your Childhood's Soundtrack

I.

Sundays belonged to Mahalia,
but Monday was Millie Jackson's day,
by Friday....

Mama's didn't know it yet,
losin one sense to gain another—
the ability to insert themselves
in between the breath and space
of each lyric that left his lips—
there was no doubt
He was sangin bout them
He was sangin to them

II.

He was singing to us, reminded us
they didn't care about us. How could
we question that? How could we
break the big he became? Giving
original meaning to the blurred lines
we were never going to question,

the same way we could never question
this truth: We never stopped looking for how
to get back. We figured if we can make
mortals into heroes and heroes into gods,
then there'd be no question...
we were all in that image of holy
Right?

III.

We can't question the holy
created by our own hand
no more than we can question
the magician who made age
slip into numbers slip
in and out of the mouths
of grown women as their

daughters went missing
Lyrics became the psalms
we repeated as we became
accomplices to our bodies
becoming ignitions, cars,
jeeps, or an endless hotel

He birthed relationships
into existence, spoke
babies into being...
How do we question
he who made us sanctified
on the dance floor?

IV.

On the dance floor is where
I would try to shuffle right,
shuffle left, buck my hips

If I buck my hips hard enough
I become him. The beat and his voice
take me back to that world premiere,

the way he re-invented the thing
we can't name. How would we ever
find anything vulgar in that?

V.

Vulgar might not come close.
It was proof turned pornography
Black girl interrupted

by viewing parties, by all the women
who said they would've taken her place
How many different ways did we all claim
it wasn't him?

VI.

Q. Did they do it?
A. That is not really the question.
How did the music make us feel
at our weddings? Graduations?
All those Saturday nights at the club?
Didn't they remind us of flying
with our feet on the ground?

Q. Did they do it?
A. When our stories went missing,
didn't we say they were the ones who
handed them back to us?

Q. Where do I put the cassette tapes,
the albums, the ....
A. Can we un-paint all the pain that's
been on the walls in the rooms
of our psyche? Can we remove all
the wallpaper from our childhoods?

Q. Where is the sin in the gods created and
crafted by human hands?
A. As gods go, they demand sacrifice.

Q. What does a sacrifice to a god look like?
A. Our daughters.
Our sons.
Ourselves.

The place in another universe teaching us our lost adolescence in a new alphabet

A. You brought back
the meaning of place
as kin, as that gathering,
as that where we may
not look alike, but we
know each other

B. Your kitchen still holds
the girl with Arachne etched
upon her right shoulder,
she stands between the old
soapstone, him, and me
I wanted to be her for his gaze,
for the way he says with his
fingertips, *I like your ink*

C. Your fireplace be big
as in real big, as in
big enough for bodies,
as in...well damn,
it heats this room for dancing

D. It heats that corner where
the lovers hide, it warms
the girl who asks for peacock feathers
in the dark, it be big enough
for the raised-right-here-hog

E. Somewhere between one
of the kitchens, one of the
living rooms, the dance
is called, the Tryin-Too-Hard-
Somewhat-Sexy-Dancing-Girls
are puttin on some kinda
show with feather boas,
but that music? Always jumpin,
always jive, live
No CDs
No iTunes

F. For those who wanna be
seen but watch, or those
who wanna watch and maybe
be seen, you have ways,
you have spaces...

G. That bump out in your
kitchen snuggles that bay window
catches the cacophony of voices
holds the wraiths of past chat,
present chat, and that talk of next
alongside the ghost of Girl-with-
Stranger-Wearin-Her-Favorite-Boots
Memba them? She laid like a child
at naptime, her face still there
buried in his chest as the first hello

H. Your kitchen table
keeps vigil over what was, will be,
and the personals. This one
on the lip of an envelope sayin,
Single, with land, with job. No kids.
Children and wife? Yeah, Sure,
I'll try it. Preferably someone who owns
a liquor store...this one answered
for the way it was so funny

I. In another part of you,
the-damn-near-room-sized-loom
In another, us singing Madonna
acoustic just because
In the yard, the girl
who climbs the tree
for the first time in ever
Years from now she'll say,
Those hippies were fairies
in an enchanted garden...
they made me do it

J. Your hall holds endless food,
the smoke from the bonfires
sticks to nose hairs, hangs on beams
like the curing raised-right-here-hog
dangles, hangs like the words of the host,
this cucumber smells like it came from the store

K. You spun giddy listenin
to the chant of can't—
I can't do "e,"
I can't do acid,
I can't with the shrooms,
pot brownie?
Your gazes always spoke
a magic turnin *No* to *Yes*,
or somethin like,
Ok, just a small piece

L. You become anybody's
anything teaching taste
like new positions for the tongue,
training the hands of naysayers sayin,
Girl, you don't cut a raised-right-here-hog
fresh from fire...do like this   with your fingers

M. You brought back
the obsolete meaning
of kindred, as in,
We been doin this before
the universe knew about
any of you

N. Brought it back like
it neva went missing,
like the way your body
be known, solace. Elixir
for the lonely, looked a lot
like proximity-turned-crush,
a lot like the way a Gandalf
doppelganger you introduced
me to did it for me   No joke

O. I keep comin back, practicing
this linguistics, a lot like
disappearing into and out of
him, him, and into holding
patterns of detachment into...
I could just keep coming back
and doing this

P. If you go,
there are rules,
rules for those
who neva been

1. Learn about it
through the mail
as in the snail kind

2. Learn about it through
those who been there,
the cashier in the bakery,
the lawyer, the girl-with-
Arachne-tattoo-etched-on-left-shoulder
walking down the street. They'll all
lean in and ask, *Are you going?*

3. Accept
Though you don't know
how you'll get there,
or how you'll get back

4. Go by way of
a house mate's car,
pay for gas.

Go by way of,
a stolen-but-not
really-stolen truck,
your friend won't
call the police

Go by way of
the lover-looking-
for-his-next-fuck-
kind of lover

Go by way of the lover-
who-wasn't-really-a-
lover-lover

Go any way you want,
just get there

5. Once there, choose your room
   once there, put your stuff on
   the bed, put *Taken* on the door

6. Do this and still run into
   the fools found naked in
   your room

7. Wake up to Dick Francis
   holding the window open
   and the hillbilly gentleman
   you been with vanished
   for his morning coffee

8. Wake up to the fiddle
   played by the ugly ass
   dude who tries to charm

9. Wake up with an apology if you
   were the fool, the naked fool,
   who stole the room the night before

Q. Leaving after the
   party doesn't end
   isn't the point

R. Get there,
   give yourself over

S. Be in the space,
give yourself over

T. Go to sleep,
wake up to...

U. or just stay sleep

V. because leaving after the party isn't the point

For here is endless

The Day God's Thermostat Broke: Ghettoclaustrophobic Dream Interlude

"This never happened.
It will shock you how much it never happened."
— Mad Men —

"The sleeper must awaken."
— Dune 1984 —

Biggie

wanted one more chance while Foxxy Brown was hoping that
someone would take her home tonight. And Spike Lee's ice cube on
Rosie's breasts in that movie imprinted like those lyrics. We all wish
we had that ice cube except our hot didn't look that cool.

Heat turned bubble gum into the lava
that never let go of the bottom of our shoes.

A reminder that God's thermostat was broke

The walkman

keeps skipping on that one song on that tape they took back to the store.
They took that tape back to the store cuz what was a child doin listening
to something that was....vulgar? My music threatens Mama's music
She's screamin from the front seat,
'I can hear it all the way from up here!'
TLC drowns out Millie Jackson.

We are captives of the backseat
Skin sticks to car seats that are somewhere between leather and plastic
The air conditioning in the car as broke as God's thermostat

McDonald's is our only hope and pinching Maurice as we
approach the golden arches is a promise
that we might get there

When God's thermostat is broken,

find other ways to keep busy
Keep away from strangers
Keep away from the places where you don't belong

Something about the way the heat brings about the more that would never cross your mind.

Also, you are never supposed to talk to strangers
let alone pick them up in your car,
well, unless you know them.
Even you know them, you don't pick them up on a summer night.
But isn't it safe if you have your friends in the car?

Wade was walking along the side of the road.
Wade had a stay off and on at that place where everyone knows...
there are secret tunnels and where they kept the patients.

You know Wade. He's always on the corner, he'll freestyle a poem.
He's always on the corner
He'll say something witty to draw you in
And those eyes...

his eyes are a kind of brown-green color not noticeable enough
to make him handsome. It wasn't just his words that made you know
where he'd been and where he was going again.
You just knew looking into his eyes.

The kind of eyes that made you peer in
The kind of eyes that spoke his crazy right into you as he talked

Speakin of crazy

Sometimes boredom has a way about it,
a kinda saunter like its twin, Trouble.

They both show up when it's hot.
See, trudgin through snow, or trying not to fall on ice
don't work to well for these two. Trouble and Boredom manifested
in a dude, the color one of the early spring flowers, color of Forsythia.

No government name, but a one-word-two-syllable street name
He was straight outta the Newport Pleasures ad
A cat with a slick look and what he bloomed we didn't want,
but like Forsythia he appeared
on time and within his season.

He made us pay attention to the way that day ate night,
the way night ate the children who had to succumb
to the endless ride in the purple Cadillac.
He made us pay attention to what happened when mamas felt the heat
of a broken thermostat when their husbands are at work.
The ghetto version of a bar hop.

He taught us that people, like houses, are interchangeable.
He taught us that like the endless tap in a bar hop,
intoxicated cars stumble like the ones who had too many Hunch Punches

And when cars stumble in the heat,
they hit telephone poles

That summer seemed to belong to us

The beach. Running in Elizabeth Park. Sitting outside of your apartment
talking about what we wanted life to be, we knew it wasn't this.

It was the summer of the divorce.
That first one where I had to wait 90 days
and five minutes for a judge to ask one question.
That one where his last words were tossed into air,
'You know? Marriage and children aren't really my thing.'

That was the day a store ate my emotions, my time, and my keys
My car was in the parking lot
The superintendents were tired of this game called,
I lost my keys.

But you were there for all of it. Seeing you soothed the loss.
We hung hard that summer like wet clothing no one bothered to ring out.
Hooland filled our ears with stories
Hooland talked shit about waiting for his checks and that story
Hooland told that one story he liked to re-tell about finding a small piece
A little somethin-somethin in the tin foil. Hooland called it coke. Imitating
the way he found it and sampled it
The way he said it was the good shit before taking another hit.

We always knew he was making it up. He never found it in your car.
It was something he just had on him, right? He liked the attention we
gave him by laughing. When we told him he made it up,
he would get more insistent. Sometimes angry.

We had to believe him

In Broken Radiators,

We trust
We trust that feel good, alright, and all sorts of wrong
be interchangeable

Something about broken radiators
and the way everyone is like to believe anything...
Like the way I tell my friends I can't stay long for a visit,
I must to go be a fairie in the woods. More like Autumn's sister at a medieval fair.

My shoes went missing like my husband.
My bare stocking feet wonder why the shoes were there in the first place,
don't they interfere with just being?

When it is hot like that, the just right kind of hot,
mothers tell their sons...'It's okay, the fairies have fairy dust.'

Other mothers forget to warn their sons,
'When you try to trick the wrong fairie son, even if it's at a fair
Trick her by asking her on a date
Fool her by asking her to pay your way
Try to be and say the things she has already heard

she won't stay and she may lead you to your doom'

The fae folk be cunning folk
Their eyes always preceed your knowing

It was the night we knew

Mother Nature threw her hands up. Mother Nature knew a good roast would teach all our asses a lesson.

Night was not for solace but good trouble.

We parked the car near of the bushes
We ignored the large orange signs—KEEP OUT/DANGER/
CLOSED FOR CONSTRUCTION
We figured they didn't mean it. The dirt road was still ours.

That dirt road, that cornfield,
us making no apologies for getting out of the car
and sauntering beyond the KEEP OUT *signs as if*
they were meant for someone else

Us walking past the cornfield as if
those big machines were warnings for someone else
Our bodies enveloped by darkness shattered by huge headlights,
they were coming for us.

We got it now, we learned our lesson
We understood now, and turned around,
the ground became our drums that we beat with our feet
Hot summer air ate our laughter,
the last laugh had by the ditch that took one of us down.

That's all how Wade happened
Picking him up on the side of the road
The idea about going into the woods and taking off our clothes
No one was looking and when God's thermostat is broken,
all of the irrational has a reason for existing

We sat around the fire holding ourselves and telling stories.
We sat around the fire,
none of us looking into Wade's eyes that night.

As he spoke, the fire seemed to bring out the nameless color of his eyes.

During that summer

Our eyes ate before our stomachs did, especially when we were at
Aunt Mary and Uncle John's house. Especially when it came
to Kentucky Fried Chicken. Family size mix of original and spicy.
The spicy for the way it is crispy, the original for the way it had that flavor.
Their secret recipe. But our recipe was something like this:

Add a Great-Aunt and a Great-Uncle
and their mustard-colored house in South Windsor
Add a mama seemingly happy until she draws her lips tight,
tighter than a cat's asshole, for an unknown reason
Add at least one child to seal this memory of how toxic thangs
only deemed toxic later in life can be confused with love

Optional ingredient: Cousins
Most important ingredient: Aunt Mary's Kool-Aid, the kind that is always too sweet
The kind that seemed to call for a five pound bag of sugar

Notice how the sweet pairs nicely with the grease on the tongue. Notice how
the fried chicken mixed with Auntie Mary's -too-sweet-for-the-teeth Kool-Aid
were the baneful bites that trained the tongue. Notice how the
trained tongue knows that the most toxic of thangs are the thangs
taste best in summer's heat

World War II

is imprinted upon the face of that building but it refuses to tell us any of its secrets. The apartment here in Naples is big. New York is all over the living room betraying the Italian spoken on the streets.

No fans. No air conditioning. Repellent discovered a few days ago Even with the repellent, they like what they tasted, they will not stop coming back for more skin. More blood.

The sun beats us down by day. By night, a breeze refuses us. The pipes hum. The television brings us oddities from the only channel that works. My favorite from the other day was an Italian music video, 'That Bastard Don't Love Me.' We like it here. The oddities. The hum. Trying to guess the connection between the layers and buildings between time.

'You are walking on bodies. On graves,' said the mother of the man who owned the apartment. Buildings built from what was found in graves. In between the space of the quiet in the apartment we wonder. Maybe she is right.

Sometimes we try the locked door thinking the apartment is as big as the one in Rosemary's Baby.

Maybe the Devil is our neighbor. Remember what a friend told us, back in the states? At one of our parties?

'If you play the right music, the Devil will come.'

Are we playing the right music?

It brought about immaculate inceptions

Going to the corner store with the neighborhood thief,
or to steal a glance at one of the fine ass Puerto Rican brothers
Long car rides to random nowhere destinations
Bodies siphoning air conditioning while posing as potential customers,
better than going to the only-park-sanctioned-by-mama-park
Endless prank calls, better than walkmen on repeat
A trip to Riverside Amusement Park?

That's the ultimate
screaming just because, talking loud, fried-dough-sugar-high-giddy...

That day,

that little girl on Harold street in the tan scarf turned halter against a pre-developed frame with bangs bringing the sound of beads into her own ears is not thinking about god's thermostat.

For her, it's not broken

She wonders if this is how heat will always feel to bare feet or skin, wonders if they all could continue like this.

If this is God's Thermostat broken personified with forever day with our voices echoing into the womb of summer....

Then fuck it,

this is the one broken thang that needs no fixin

III.

Trying to Speak Woman in My Own Tongue

Cthulhu's Diaries

I.
Knee high brown socks is the last thing I remember,
did it all start in the basement?

The way an elementary school bathroom stall
holds the secrets of playing house like

the way a whistle makes contact with yellow
shorts fitted upon pre-pubescent bodies

Somewhere in a dark living room, your ice cream
lands my 9-year-old legs, somewhere,

barely hidden by the lip of the doorway, that boy
is still waiting. He's next. Looked a lot like

the night I wanted to scream at the ceiling,
I'M NOT READY, a lot like ignoring the way

the veins strained against his neck, never noticing
her resistance on my nightstand. I kept thinking

Klimt's kiss could bring me more of that thang.
I once hoped that school children finished what I

started with a wish bone after they understand banter
on a playground, before they realize that full moons

will keep minding their own business with or without
your words. Against the concrete walls, he dry-fucked me

in Auntie's garage while homemade vanilla ice
cream dripped down our chins. I wanted his hands

on my 8-year-old body. They warned, *He feels you up,
everyone knows it.* I spent all my Harold Street

waiting for it, like trying to decipher the first sounds
of the universe. Knees digging into mats, clasps hands

are better than the ones pumping fists. All just another
way to say meditation, yoga, Tantra, Sutras, Confession?

Like a lost child with beads between my fingers, I chanted
Om Mani Padme Om, killing you before your eyes could open

I didn't have an apology big enough for that invitation.

II.
No apology big enough

for that invitation,

so I killed you before your eyes could open
chanting *Om Mani Padme Om*

like a lost child

holding beads between my fingers...

meditation, yoga, tantra,

sutras,

all to say
clasped hands are better than the ones pumping fists

Knees dug into mats

tried to decipher the first sounds of the universe
like spending all my Harold Street waiting

though they warned,

He feels you up, everyone knows it

I wanted his hands

on my 8-year-old body

Homemade vanilla ice cream dripped down our chins

while he dry-fucked me,

I liked it.

Once, I hoped that school children could finish what I started

with a wish bone

After they understand

banter on a playground

before they realize

full moons will mind their own business with or without your words

I thought Klimt's kiss on my nightstand

could bring me more of that thang

never noticing her resistance,

ignoring the way the veins strained against his neck

Looked a lot like the night I screamed at the ceiling

I'M NOT READY

Somewhere,

that boy waited

barely hidden by the lip of the doorway

Somewhere,

He'd be next.

In the same place

where your ice cream lands

on my 9-year-old legs in a dark living room.

Like the way a whistle makes contact with yellow shorts.

The way an elementary school bathroom stall
holds the secrets of playing house.

Or did it all start in that basement?

The last thing I remember is knee high brown socks...

Girl Child

Girl child run wild, wild girl child
left her trail of scent behind. Child
don't you know about the boys? Girl child
wild ignorance will last so long, child
don't you know? That polish, chile
those beads, that scarf turned halter child,

only gonna get you trouble! Child
Remember Ebony? She had a child
and barely a child herself, and girl child
Mrs. kitchen abortions, Chiiiilllle,
the nails, the hangers, left road to ruin, child
runnin wild hope you know what you doin, child

did you see? Your own mama, chile
she a tale flashin her tail. That chile
earned motherhood too early child
Forget the boys! Barbie's a safer bet. Child,
forget anything about being cute child.
Forget playin house. Remember Tanya chile?

That ain't a life, but what is? Girl child?
Child no longer, budded breasts bloom, Chile
no period arrived here yet, but gurllll, chiillle,
She a damned handful! Wild girl child
nature might slow you down. Girl child
runnin wild those streets will fuck you up. Chile,

remember your own mama child?
That might not be your papa.Chile,
you needed someone to teach you child
lead you girl child, well look here chile,
I guess it's on you, on your shoulders girl child
part woman. Don't show so many teeth, chile!

Make sure those breasts don't bob, chile
put powder in the right place. Chile
stop that natural twitch. Girl part child
walk slower, it'll slow the path of scent. Chile,
don't make eye contact with those mens. Chile,
no need to say hello to everyone chile

Before you leave your parents, child
do you know? Girl, woman, child, chile, oooh chiillllle

It's a cash register, you better know how to use it.

Trying to Speak Woman

because, I be bride,
sometimes, I be taken...

My hunger produces
lost friends, apartments,
their hunger expands
into labyrinths

I am rebirthed by
First Lust and Jealousy
Here, I be a xenophobe
estranged from

adapting to their
custom, their
language. My body
as wonderland,

as kept, as what
happens to me
while I've gone
missing

Me as their Minotaur,
an exotic of their
imagining

The children of Lack & Plenty
have nothin on me

Lessons in Development from a Butterfly

Egg

At 5, my favorite yellow dress rips,
a first lesson in how the body betrays.
Barbie's body, the first way we
learn what the adults are doing.
At 6, I am introduced to butterflies
by the way adults spread their legs

when they want something. A man
visiting flashes his butterfly legs,
no face or voice, folds his body to my level
hovering on a threshold. *Go ahead,* they
say, *give it to him*, they say as the erosion
of the bridge between gimme and mine
becomes the tongue of girlhood.
This long before a faceless woman with

the same butterfly legs. This time, her
yellow meat exposed by black shorts
I remember because of the way she holds
court amid mothers and children. Let me
see, she'll demand. Putting me on the road
to be somebody's *Pretty Baby*. T-shirts

will be no more a protection than mothers
and witnesses who collude encouraging,
Go ahead, teaching how to memorize

the answer to this question:
Is this what a hug means in their language?

Butterflies are nature's first lesson in deception.
The first memory that beauty, like the adults in the
human world, can be trusted.

Larva

At 7, my body becomes a playscape.
Playing house gone wrong in dark closets,
locked porches, all versions of oblivious
babysitters. I become trained to the stares
that pounce pon mouths to conceal touch,
the same way mouths learn that naming

how his whistle hit my ass through smoke, a torn
fence, and amid his boys won't earn protection.
Instead, the adults ask, *Show us how you were walking?*
At 9, something like this...a walk turned run while
being chased around a tree, avoiding the growing
pile of hugs, kisses, and butterfly legs while
a second-grade class line stands still.
The teacher watches, silently saying *boys will be boys*

Walk turned run, this time running up a hill.
He pins me the way a dog pins its bone
while his older sister watches. No kicking
or screaming get doors to open nor anyone to
believe. Is this what the other he meant when
he said he'd *get* me?

In this stage, some kinds eat their siblings,
some kinds mimic royalty to become the
Queen in the center of an ant colony,
celebration turned massacre.

Pupa

At 12, all trick, no treat and the Easter
Bunny's gone missing the way tan scarfs
turned halter tops, and the cut denims
have gone missing like all the things that
made me feel brown body beautiful.
Substituted with the fuzzy, salmon

colored bathrobe with a broken zipper
to conceal shame. Gym socks when pads
have run out, the long, cotton tube kind
to hide the proof. Add the month that slips
into two months plus the years it takes

to become fluent in secrets, bilingual in lying,
and silence. At 13, that age when I discover
there is no elixir for hunger, no reason for the
road dissolving between want and un-want,
or the way brown body beautiful is found through
his, his, and his lips. The beginning of sexual

apprenticeship—Pay attention! A smile and
flirting gets extra deli meat. A sway of hips
and glimpse of daughter? A street vendor's
discount on t-shirts. Allow a picture to be
taken in some strange man's apartment who
is not your husband? Priceless...

At this stage, some encounter a pupal
rape trapped within her chrysalis
with no choice but to mate during this
in-between state.

Adult

If you don't set the price for your pussy,
someone else will. It's worth extra meat,
a discount, worth free food stamps, maybe
gold, maybe a rabbit fur coat. It may be
worth the things you can afford to buy yourself
At some age unknown, they all   look the same

questions, was-bands, the moments
of being the bone that refuses to stop
singing. The same blur of guests who ask,
Was she good? Sometimes they'll be the
boy in the bar with a fixed glare who
is really saying, *I'm going to get you.*
Glares and all the ways legs became butterfly
wings pinned open travelling at the speed of

time passing multiplied by dark closets that
become rooms, beds, plus the body that betrays.
Always the body that betrays by attracting attention.
This time, I teach myself how to say gimme
This time, I am fluent in
No
Mines
You can't have

*If one makes it this far, she can dine off blood,
the sweat of others, or tears. BEWARE, these
butterflies emerge from their chrysalis as trained
experts in survival.*

Ghettoclaustrophobic Dreaming of Husbands, of Children

I'm somewhere asking answers of questions I already know
Asking a woman in Georgetown, *explain the maps on my palms to me*
A marriage she said, two children she said, but the house? Never spoken
along with her silent disclaimer—*Leaving here could change all that*

I'm somewhere asking a woman in Rhode Island, *Explain those cards*
Maybe marriage, babies...maybe, but speak of houses never leave her lips
along with her silent disclaimer *A fool can do anything to change that*
I build a map of how it was all supposed to be using bone dust and braille

Marriages, babies, expand, become sprawling houses designed in forgotten
I'm somewhere asking a Zion street witch, more seers, more tarot, I-Ching
I'm the cartographer of how it's all supposed to be using bone dust and braille
as if I know all of these places better than all of the They who explain it to me

I'm somewhere asking witches, more seers, more tarot, reading the I-Ching
trained in haunting psyches and embedding embers, they leave a trail of ash
I follow the trail as if I know better than all of the They who tell it to me
they knew better, trained in the way hope goes missing like the lines on palms

Trained in haunting psyches, they embed embers, and leave a trail of ash
somewhere, I will appear. I will keep asking about every place I've been
They know better, trained in the way things go missing like lines on palms,
all the faces of the tarot. No knowing, no seeing can create what never was

Somewhere, I will appear, I will keep asking about every place I've been
Marriages they'll say, *babies* they'll sneer, houses will never be spoken
All the faces of the tarot go missing like their knowing and seeing
I'm someplace darning half-truths out of answers to questions I already know

IIII

Fugue-Woke-State

When the Imagined Become More Real or Something Like...

a sinister halo birthing one
then two then something like three
they wanted my motive more than
wanting to expose the girl behind the shouting

More than the way it created
a sinister kind of halo in an abandoned lot
in the hour that pretends seven
I battle with Nyx and Reason

One, two
then something like three
it was now two years ago
300 miles ago, Detroit A Black man stands on the street corner

We go into the coffee shop
We see that man shouting
Something my eyes couldn't hear
He needs a pencil

Refuse, I say
Lie if you have to, I instruct
I am giving birth to a sinister halo
I can't hear the tale,

It was about a job, in this area hires people
and they don't pay them, happened to my daughter
The once there is here
I am a Black woman shouting in a parking lot

Opening my trunk
I am asking for that pencil
from those who spin like solar systems
lights beam into empty lot

See how they watch you open a trunk
those sinister halos oh how they light a lot
Oh how they bounce
off Black skin at night

In Fugue Woke States of In-Between

It was really an asylum
They forced us to say

what getting out means,
we tell them, *we gonna set*

boundaries. Anotha speak
for protection circles, a kinda

speak for we set boundaries to
break others. In the shadow of the

street lights that never go out—
280 Collins Street, in Mama's lap, in

wherever all things gone missing be—
it wasn't about any of these places, but

how well you be walking backwards counting
all the things between wake, fugue, and

woke, how well you be multilingual
in signs, fluent in breaking silences,

gain mastery in transmutation, most
important, can you be trickster incarnate?

The mirror reflecting what the world thinks it sees?

That Which Can't Be Measured

INGREDIENTS

- *3 bodies bullet free celebratin graduation*
- *3 blood aunties and 2 extended aunties. The two that go back before youngins took up residence in a womb. Before we knew a now*
- *Add uncles*
- *Add the sizzle on the grill of the meat refusing time*
- *2 orange like really orange peppers*
- *1 ½ red peppers*
- *1 ½ green peppers*
- *1 yellow pepper*

PREPARATION

Cut the celery like this...to fit in the hand and the mouth. Save one pepper for each of the platters to core, they will hold the ranch dressing. They will be the center piece. Remember color balance. The orange-really-orange-pepper should balance with the celery, green pepper, red pepper. The tomatoes? Yes rinse! Place them between the green, the orange, but not next to the red. The baby carrots, they fit as is no choppin needed.

When we do the fruit salad—be careful. Rinse this chopping board don't use the other. Keep the baby melon whole while coring. Take those peeled oranges and chop like this. Add red seedless grapes, six sliced up oranges, chop the flesh from the melon. Chewable bite sized. Let the juices meld.

Add the teenager in the corner who hung out too late with his older cousins. Leave long enough to pour boiling water and light sternos. Leave long enough to allow time to calm wind. Maybe ask for help. Return. Juices melded. Fill the mini melon with the fruit, fill the pineapple.

A dash of the girl who said she had no friends. One of the aunts-not-blood aunts who says she's the youngest of all four of us sayin, *These youngins tell me things I don't repeat.* Whatever you do, don't forget the table. The table not too big, not too small in the room with the boiling pots, in the room with the kettle about to scream.

Leave enough room for all the choppin, this is important. A board barely big enough for all the juices. Don't forget the bowl in the drainer almost your age according to Grandma. Wash the knife in cold water says Grandma *They keep mi knives sharp*, she says, *Ya learn something every day,* she chants.

2 Grandmas—one double-deep-chocolate, one color of coffee-double-cream—sprinkled with asks for fruit garnished with watchful eyes, questions, wisdom, and one vanilla bean girl. A specific vanilla bean with the same name as Auntie. She stands beside you among grandmas, entering and exiting aunties, and Nani's crazy ass lecturing you about having children sayin, *You know you could get a surrogate.*

Don't forget the girl, the one girl who moves Auntie-with-the-same-name-as-vanilla-bean to declare, *Mi spirit tek you.*

Curatorial Tags for the Exhibition:

What Home Means When People,
Places, and Things Go Missing
Between Wake and Sleep

I. Harold Street (c.1988)

Harold street, the childhood home for
a hot sec, the hot sec before getting out.
Something about a guy, about the house.
The first time I learn houses, like people,
go missing

II. Index of Items and People Lost (I) (c.1988)

Erase a grandmother, aunts, cousins
from the second and third floors.
Pack roller skates, the brass beds,
Vietnam photo albums, Dr. Seuss,
Beatrix Potter, wedding photos,
the bubble gum pink robe, the first loaded
gun ever held by my six-year-old hands...

III. Index of Items and People Lost (II) (c.1988)

and the cabbage patch kids, Christie Lola
and Spencer. Pack with no explanation.
Doing what they say makes everything easier.
Memory teaches code breaking training
the tongue in questions that become
taste buds never exposed to air

IV. A Week of Unexplained Family Time at Howard Johnson's (c.1988)

Howard Johnson wasn't a family
vacation, yet we had all our stuff.
Where does all the clothing go with
no dresser drawers? Their creamers soothing
to the tongue of one who doesn't know

V. Index of Items and People Lost (III) (c.1988)

The Black-Eyed peas, the clown cup
once filled with grandma's banana pudding,
the hamster, the fish, the record player,
"Boogie Wonderland," Model Market,
the Pitbull named Shogun, Mr. Thomas's
store, all take up residence in a place no longer

VI. Untitled (c.1988-89)

Howard Johnson's became the hotel
on the pike, birth of the glow from the
television screen that spoke soothing,
and the smells that trained my nose,
my spirit to avoid the vernacular of poverty

VII. Index of Items and People Lost (IV) (c. 1988-89)

Hotels traded for Wanda's one room,
the place made awesome cause Church's Chicken
is across the street. Wanda-Mama's-childhood-
friend-reuse-the-bathtub-water-Wanda.
Wanda's, where more things gone missing
like daddy's pants, like

VIII. Index of Items and People Lost (V) (c.1989 – 90)

the one car that carries all our stuff. Something
about a mickey in a drink, something about
a room, a woman...Wanda's exchanged for
Auntie and Uncle's basement eventually traded up
for our own place, an apartment at 280 Collins Street

IX. Index of Items and People Lost/New Items for New Home (VI) (c.1989 – 90)

Me, mine, own...quietly went missing
No one ever says what any of this is or was
I become a pedagogical expert in
If it isn't named, if it isn't spoken,
then it didn't really happen,
a cartographer of silences, the lost,
white spaces,   the abandoned,   stolen,
the forgotten

X. Untitled (c.1990)

Speaking detachment becomes
no movement, no fad, but
a forced native tongue involving
a monastic life, holding vigil
and caretaking the reliquary
for all things gone missing

To the Valley of the Lost Pharaohs

I.

Some say it was *Om*, some say the first
sound eva was *Yo*. Others are inclined to
believe it was a mother humming loud enough
to get her children to come back sayin, *Come back.*
if you can't come back, remember your names.
Here, she be like Mama Evans of Good Times.

Here, there be no movie set, no cameras,
no play-play. No staging. It was apartment
207, maybe 3 something. Each of 'em
a fade, the kind of do tapered tight on the
sides, a drop of Big Daddy Kane, a touch
of curl within that mane. The gold, cheekbones
that cut through the uncertainty, cut through
any question, any doubt...*I know you*
If this be a museum, save the curatorial tags

II.

I know you in the way I need no maps,
no arrows, guards, or anythang to remind
me of the way I remember how the walk
lacking limp meant that the real ones
didn't need all that. High top fades atop
different shades of anyone's any kind
of chocolate. The way you remained a
young girl's crush, the way ya'll reminded
older women of the passion drained away
from the ones they waited for. Like the
way the hood committed the sin of
transmutation upon skin that looked
like that. Bricks piled high colliding with
air, concrete and scene Cloaked Griots

spinning stories like vinyl except this
time, those be stories of what never was,
but what became. You can't keep a dead
kingdom dead forever, you can separate
a people from their kingdom but they'll find it
Thrones now blocks masquerading

III.

as fiefdoms to those who know the difference
deep somewhere The same those who lack limp
stand the way their mama's taught 'em, walk the
ways their papas taught 'em cause *They gon find*
a reason to say they don't believe... You
and all your brothers, like every otha

brotha, got no choice in trading kingdoms,
stuck wit these blocks. Yet, you walk
that way forcing us to say, *I know you.*
In the way that only DNA sees
DNA, in the way one tries to find another,
in the way that the brown stranger on a
bar stool once said, *Even if I don't know*
you, even if you be up to no good,

I need to get close to you. An echo
birthing the question: If a piece is broken
from the whole, can it ever remember what
it felt like before the crack? Before the split?
Even the Yo from the first Yo eva heard
knows it found itself sounding off building

IV.

in concrete jungles. A mother's lullaby tangled
in the sound that found its way into the
ears of these lost who knew that
told they missing

We Got...

Language. Whether Northeast, South,
West Coast, West Indies...we throw signs
How the call of a full name signals trouble,
the bow of branches mimicking a Weeping

Willow soundin like the voices that be
a distant home like the way a street holds
our childhoods, cradling our stupidity,
secrets, our first discovery of brown body

beautiful like that summer mama turned
headscarves into halter tops. Then, New York
was just a place on a salmon-colored-tube-top
that caught the eye of the drunk-corner-bums

We couldn't escape blood, memory,
the virility of nostalgia like the way a porch
can go missing for years, yet we memba it as
theater, as watch tower, as that place where

White Larry stood in his army whites. Where
mamas and extended aunties traded gossip
like recipes, where fingers colluded with hot
combs and jars of *Blue Magic* transmitting hope

to thick manes of little Black girls who sent
prayers to the Patron Saint of Good Hair hopin that
kinky coils be turned glory be turned to crowns of
cornrows and beads, or *Maybe my hair be like Ebony's*

hair at school. We not stardust, we be the stars
doin time in our cluster spread across a womb
lengthened by the centuries pregnant with all the good
we forgot. It's the stories that make us shine, combined

with stolen, lost, forgotten, found, and the knowing: We
were neva among the missing, jus the faint marks of erased
between white spaces. We be the alchemists, the meaning
of magician, fashioning ourselves from the wreckage of memory

Wake: A Spell

Body pitched to the unseen

Don't darn all the holes,
leave some for the looking.

Don't say all that is seen,
leave some for those who gonna say...

Wake

escaped
walls and mouths gonna say otherwise

Between wake and sleep, some gonna ask you,
?

Between wake and sleep, some gonna dare you,
You are the one who checked in here

No need to tell you

Wake

Yours is a tongue tuned to tellin
stitch stories
darn trauma
weave joy

And for the unwritten   the neva said,
the neva seen...

Raise up as if dead

ACKNOWLEDGMENTS

These acknowledgments are not in order of hierarchy because all these places and individuals helped in creating this work.

My gratitude to the following publications that featured some of these pieces: *Palette Poetry* and *ITERANT Literary Magazine*.

My deep gratitude and appreciation to my husband, MacLean Charles Gander, for encouraging my voice and for being one of my harshest critics. You continue to push me to not just be better, but great.

My gratitude to Magdelena Gomez and the podcast *Jazz Ready* which featured me reading "Black Book of Creation" and "Trying to Speak Woman."

My gratitude to Kahywanda Wilson. You have always shared the experience of your family with me and I am grateful for the way that the spirit and richness of you and your family inspired "That Which Can't Be Measured."

Similarly, a thanks to members of my extended family: Sarah Bowen Chinue Clifford, Jasminum McMullen, Pamela Moore, Desmond Peeples, Kelli Perkins, Nikyda Resto, Kristen Sadowski, Andrea Shader, and so many others who gave their time, ear, and enduring support by listening and encouraging me to boldly be in the world with all my work.

My Vermont College of Fine Arts family and my previous advisers who have provided me with many insights that still light my path. My additional gratitude to Philip Metres for encouraging me to put my work into the world.

My gratitude to Ruth Antoinette Rodriguez, also within my extended family as a dear friend, fellow poet, and enduring curator who has created a truly literary space at Antidote Books. Thank you for all the ways that you have invited me to put my work out into the world.

My gratitude to Donald Mutebi who continues to spend many hours putting some of these poems to music and for inspiring "Black Book of Creation" through our conversations.

My continued thanks to this group of special poets: Owen Andrews, Cynthia Gomez, Andy McCord, and Michael Ruby. All of you continue to encourage my thinking about revision, you inspire me to continue to ask the timeless and audacious questions about poetry, and you continue to provide invaluable feedback on my work.

And to Cynthia, Ed Burke, Michael, and Pam, my endless appreciation for the way you all read this manuscript cover-to-cover when it was just a shadow of what it is now. You all jumped into the pages with excitement, encouragement, and insights.

Not last, certainly not least, my gratitude to my ancestors. To the living ones and the ones no longer physically here, I am because of all of you.

No poet, writer, or artists can do anything in true solitude or alone. My thanks to all who continually help me to become.

Shanta Lee Gander is an artist and multi-faceted professional. Her endeavors include writing and photography with work that has been featured in *PRISM, ITERANT Literary Magazine, Palette Poetry, BLAVITY, DAME Magazine, The Crisis Magazine, Rebelle Society,* on the *Ms.* Magazine Blog, and on a former radio segment *Ponder This.* Shanta Lee's photojournalism has been featured on Vermont Public Radio (VPR.org) and her investigative reporting has been in *The Commons* weekly newspaper covering Windham County,VT. Shanta Lee is the 2020 recipient of the Arthur Williams Award for Meritorious Service to the Arts. Her contributing work on an investigative journalism piece for *The Commons* received a New England Newspaper & Press Association (NENPA) 2019 award. Shanta Lee gives lectures on the life of Lucy Terry Prince, considered the first known African-American poet in English literature, as a member of the Vermont Humanities Council Speakers Bureau and is the 2020 gubernatorial appointee to their board of directors.

Shanta Lee is an MFA candidate in Creative Non-Fiction and Poetry at the Vermont College of Fine Arts. She has an MBA from the University of Hartford and an undergraduate degree in Women, Gender and Sexuality from Trinity College. To see more of Shanta Lee's work, visit Shantaleegander.com.